JOHN W. SCHAUM presents

CZERNY IN ALL KEYS

For PIANO or ORGAN

Book One

FOREWORD

This unique compilation *condenses* familiar Czerny etudes into one-page studies and also *transposes* them into the 24 major & minor keys. Choices have been excerpted from a broad cross-section of Czerny's works so that all types of keyboard technic are included. Thus the student gets the time-honored benefits of Czerny technic *plus* the experience of playing in all keys.

As a supplement, the 24 major and minor scales and chords are carefully fingered and edited for the aid of the student. These appear on pages 16-17 and 30-31.

The exercises are grouped in cycle-of-keys sequence with major and relative minor keys on the *same page spread*. This enables the student to easily understand how major and minor keys are related (i.e. having the same key signature).

Because these studies are short (just 16 measures each) they offer great flexibility for assignment and increase student motivation by creating short units which are easily completed.

EXCLUSIVELY DISTRIBUTED BY

HAL•LEONARD®
CORPORATION
7777 W. BLUEMOUND RD. P.O. BOX 13819 MILWAUKEE, WI 53213

Contents Book One

Contents Book Two

Music to Correlate with the Level Two Curriculum
Making Music at the Piano, Level 2 or Piano for Adults, Level 2

THEORY:
Scale Speller
Easy Keyboard Harmony, Bk 1
Rhythm Workbook, Level 2
TECHNIC:
Fingerpower, Level 2
Technic Tunes, Book 1

CHRISTMAS:
Christmas Festival
Christmas Solos, Level 2
REPERTOIRE:
Repertoire Highlights, Level 2
Classics:
Classic Themes, Bk 1

Music for Fun:
Easy Boogie, Bk 1
Rhythm & Blues, Bk 1
Sports & Games
Stephen Foster Favorites

(See page 32 for sheet music solos)

Carl Czerny was born in Vienna, February 21, 1791, of Bohemian parentage, the name signifying "black." His father was a highly-esteemed pianist, and the little fellow came into contact with the leading artists of Vienna, including Beethoven, who gave him instructions for several years. He showed great talent for composition as well as piano playing and at the early age of fourteen, began to teach. During his long career as a teacher, which activity covered a period of more than fifty years, he had many distinguished pupils, among whom may be noted Liszt, Thalberg, Jaell, Leopold von Meyer and Leschetizky. He left a handsome fortune to Vienna charities.

He was a prolific composer, his last set of studies bearing the opus number, 848. In addition to this long list with "opus," he made arrangements of all Beethoven's Symphonies, most of those by Haydn, Mozart and Spohr, many oratorios, and an edition of Bach's "Well-Tempered Clavichord." Besides studies, his compositions include symphonies, masses, requiems and other music for the church service. In his etudes the special point is the development of the hand from the standpoint of technic. He lays aside all attempt at expression until position and independence of the fingers have been acquired.

Czerny may be literally described as a "wandering composer," for one of his publishers (Haslinger) states that he had four high desks in his room and that, in order to save time, he filled two sheets at the first desk, then did the like at the second, and so forth, so that by the time the sheets on the fourth desk were finished those on the first desk had had the necessary time in which to dry. This seems entirely credible in view of the large number of his works, in particular his many sets of studies. Czerny lived almost constantly in Vienna, until his death on July 15, 1857, making few trips and devoting his days chiefly to teaching, reserving his evenings for composition.

To show Czerny's position as a medium between the Classical School as represented by Beethoven and the Modern School, we give the following:

BEETHOVEN
teacher of
CZERNY
teacher of
LISZT and **LESCHETIZKY**

❦ ❦ ❦

1. C Major

DIRECTIONS: Do not lift the hand at the end of each slur. The purpose of the slur is to show the similarity of patterns and to indicate phrases. Follow this procedure throughout the book. The only time to release the hand at the end of a slur is when a staccato mark is used as in the study on page 14.

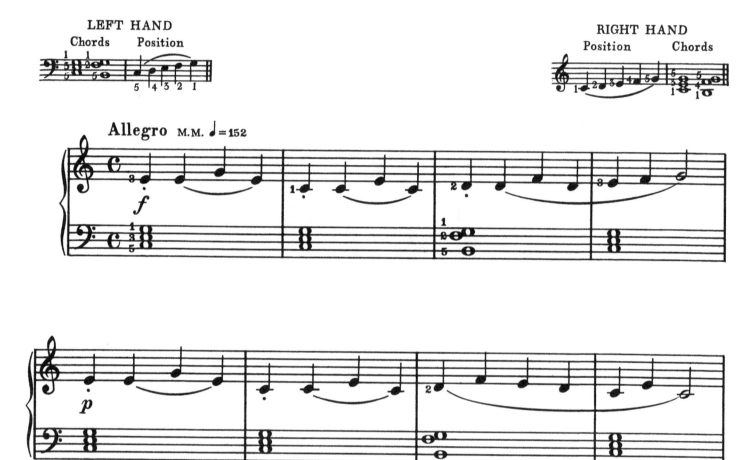

2. A Minor

3. G Major

Left Hand Position

Right Hand Position

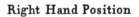

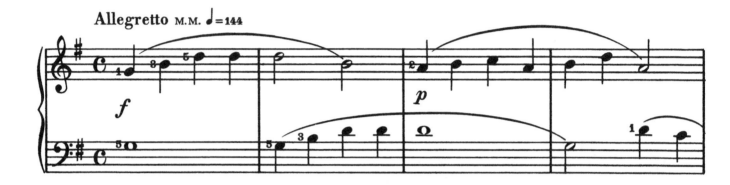

4. E Minor

5. D Major

Left Hand Patterns

Tempo di Valse M.M. ♩ = 138

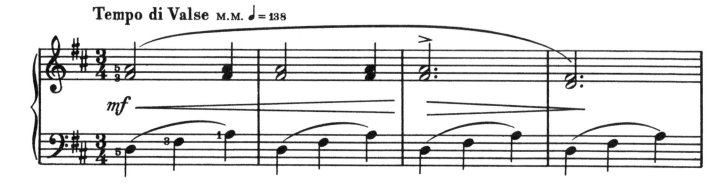

6. B Minor

Left Hand Patterns

Right Hand Position

Tempo di Valse M.M. ♩ = 138

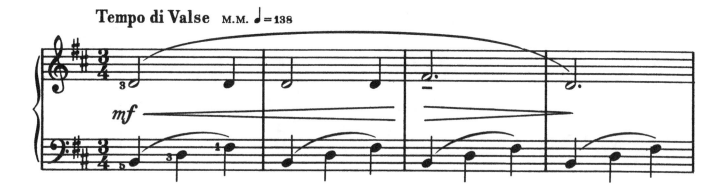

7. A Major

Left Hand Position

Right Hand Position

Con moto M.M. ♩=138

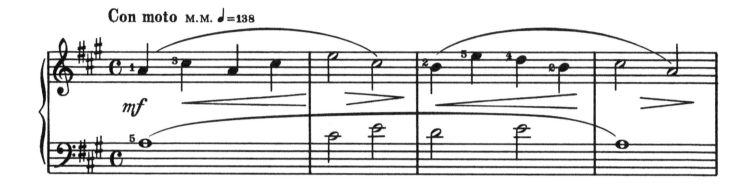

8. F♯ Minor

9. E Major

Left Hand Position  Right Hand Position

10. C♯ Minor

LEFT HAND
Chords Position

RIGHT HAND
Position Chords

Misterioso M.M. ♩=132

11. B Major

Left Hand Patterns

Right Hand Position

12. G# Minor

Left Hand Patterns

Right Hand Position

Moderato M.M. ♩ = 126

Double sharp (raises a note already sharped, another half step.)

Scales and Chords in Sharp Keys

C Major

A minor (Harmonic)

G Major

E minor (Harmonic)

D Major

B minor (Harmonic)

A Major

F# minor (Harmonic)

E Major

C# minor (Harmonic)

B Major

G# minor (Harmonic)

13. F Major

14. D Minor

15. B♭ Major

16. G Minor

17. E♭ Major

LEFT HAND
Chords   Position

RIGHT HAND
Position   Chord

Animato M.M. ♩ = 116

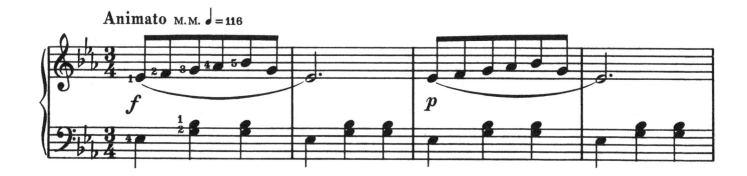

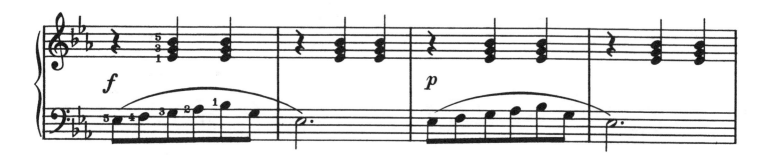

18. C Minor

19. A♭ Major

LEFT HAND
Chords   Position

RIGHT HAND
Position   Chords

20. F Minor

LEFT HAND
Chords   Position

RIGHT HAND
Position   Chords

21. D♭ Major

LEFT HAND
Chords   Position

RIGHT HAND
Position   Chords

Con brio M.M. ♩ = 138

22. B♭ Minor

Left Hand Position

Right Hand Position

28

23. G♭ Major

Left Hand Position

Right Hand Position

Vivo M.M. ♩ = 144

24. E♭ Minor

Scales and Chords in Flat Keys

Ab Major

F minor (Harmonic)

Db Major

Bb minor (Harmonic)

Gb Major

Eb minor (Harmonic)

Successful Schaum Sheet Music

This is a Partial List — Showing Level 2 and selected Level 3

• = Original Form * = Big Notes ✓ = Chord Symbols

ACTION SOLOS

55-26 •	WATER SLIDE (Staccato)	Payne	2

AMERICAN – PATRIOTIC SOLOS

55-14	AMERICA THE BEAUTIFUL	Ward	2
58-30 ✓	ANCHORS AWEIGH	Zimmerman	3
58-44 ✓	CAISSONS SONG (U.S. Field Artillery)		3
55-41 ✓	MARINE'S HYMN	Traditional	2
58-45 ✓	SEMPER FIDELIS (U.S. Marines)	Sousa	3
55-62	STAR-SPANGLED BANNER (Easy)		2
58-18 ✓	STAR-SPANGLED BANNER	Commemorative Ed.	3
55-61	STARS and STRIPES FOREVER (Easy)		2
61-13	YANKEE DOODLE	Theme & Variations	3
58-10 ✓	YOU'RE A GRAND OLD FLAG	Cohan	3

ANIMALS and BIRDS

58-62 •	BARNYARD BUDDIES	Costley	3
58-56 •	BUCKING BRONCO (L.H. Melody)	King	3
55-54 •	EQESTRIAN PROCESSION	Cahn	2
55-09 *•	POPPO the PORPOISE (L.H. Melody)	Littlewood	2

BOTH HANDS in TREBLE CLEF

55-56 •	MUSIC BOX LULLABY	Levin	2
55-44 •	MYSTICAL ETUDE (Staccato)	Cahn	2

BOOGIE

58-05 •	BEACH BALL BOOGIE	Schaum	3
55-07 *•	COOL SCHOOL (Boogie Style)	Schaum	2
55-05	HAWAIIAN WARRIOR'S DANCE	Traditional	2
55-02 •	LITTLE DOG BOOGIE	Schaum	2

CHRISTMAS

71-07	DUET: HARK THE HERALD ANGELS SING	Mendelssohn	2

CIRCUS

55-39 •	CIRCUS PONIES	Leach	2
55-58 •	CLOWN WALTZ	Kitchen	2
58-42 •	GREASE PAINT GERTIE	McKinley	3
55-53 •	RINGMASTER'S MARCH	Cahn	2

CLASSICS

58-24 *	Bach	JOY PRELUDE ("Jesu Joy of Man's Desiring")	3
58-39	Beethoven	7th SYMPHONY (2nd Mvt. Theme)	3
55-30	Mozart	ROMANCE (from "A Little Night Music")	2
58-15	Mozart	SYMPHONY No. 40 (First Theme)	3
55-45	Pachelbel	CANON (Easy Edition)	2
58-34	Salieri	MINUET IN D	3

COUNTRY/WESTERN

58-38	AMERICAN INDIAN SUITE	4 Tribal Themes	3
55-35	DAGGER DANCE ("Land of Sky Blue Waters")	Herbert	2
58-33 *✓	YELLOW ROSE, The	Traditional	3

DESCRIPTIVE MUSIC

58-48 •	COUNTY FAIR	Leach	3
55-47 •	DOMINOES	Cahn	2
55-49 •	IN A FAR OFF TIME & PLACE	Revezoulis	2
55-51 •	PEACEFUL INTERLUDE	Holmes	2
58-53 •	PERPETUAL MOTION (6/8 Time)	Cahn	3
58-60 •	PIANO PIZAZZ	Cahn	3
58-47 •	SLEEPY ALARM CLOCK	Cahn	3

ETHNIC MUSIC

55-46	COME BACK TO SORRENTO	deCurtis	2
58-07 ✓	HAVA NAGILA (Minor Key)	Israeli Folk Dance	3

HALLOWEEN

55-40 *•	GALLOPING GHOSTS (Minor Key)	Weston/Schaum	2
58-41 •	GHOSTLY JIVE (Minor Key)	Leach	3
55-57 •	TRICK OR TREAT PARADE	Rita	2
58-59 •	WACKY WITCHES	King	3

JAZZ / RAGTIME / SWING

58-19 •	COUNTRY ROCK (Jazz Style)	Jones	3
55-48 •	DUDE (Jazz Style)	Weston	3
55-21 *✓	ENTERTAINER (Easy)	Joplin	2
80-08 ✓	IN THE MOOD (Jazz Style)	Garland	3
58-51 •	RAMBLIN' RAG	King	3
55-55 •	RICKETY RAG	Schaum	2
58-57 •	RUNAROUND ROCK	Biel	3
55-59 •	SWINGIN' IN STYLE	Goodridge	2

LEFT-HAND MELODY

55-50 •	SCOTTISH SKETCH	Holmes	2

MARCHES

55-06	PARADE of the TOY SOLDIERS	Jessel	2
58-50 ✓	WASHINGTON POST MARCH	Sousa	3

MINOR KEY

55-52 •	DREAM CATCHER (Minor Key)	Holmes	2
58-43 *•	DRIZZLY DAY (Minor Key)	Holmes	3
58-49 •	SUMMER SCHERZO (Staccato)	Leach	3

MOVIE THEME

80-02	OVER THE RAINBOW (from "Wizard of Oz")	Arlen	3
80-01	STAR WARS (Main Title)	Williams	2

ROMANTIC MOOD

58-31	ASPIRATION	Schumann	3
58-01 ✓	FASCINATION WALTZ	Marchetti	3
58-36 ✓	LET ME CALL YOU SWEETHEART	Friedman	3

SACRED

55-25 *✓	HOW GREAT THOU ART	Swedish Folk Melody	2
58-32 ✓	JUST A CLOSER WALK WITH THEE	Spiritual	3

SHOW TUNES

80-21 ✓	SEND IN THE CLOWNS	Sondheim	3

SHOWY DISPLAY SOLOS

55-44	MYSTICAL ETUDE (Both Hands in Treble)	Cahn	2
55-20 *	POGO STICK CHOP (Based on "Chop Sticks")	Schaum	2
55-34 •	RIGHT ON (Staccato)	Miller	2
58-23 *•	SKATEBOARD (Cross Hands)	Schaum	3

SPORTS / LEISURE

55-64 •	CHA-CHA-CHA	Leach	2
55-43 •	ROLLER BLADES	Schaum	2
55-28 ✓	TAKE ME OUT TO THE BALL GAME	Von Tilzer	2

SPRINGTIME

58-52 •	APRIL WALK	Levin	3
55-18 *•	FAWN'S LULLABY	Masson	2

STACCATO

55-23 *•	FRISKY FROG (Both Hands in Treble)	Cahn	2
58-55 •	TANGO PIZZICATO	Cahn	3

SYNCOPATION

58-54 •	SOMBRERO	Cahn	3
58-58 •	WEST INDIES FESTIVAL	King	3

THANKSGIVING

55-12	THANKSGIVING SCENE	Medley of 4 Hymns	2

WALTZES

55-37 •	PICTURE POSTCARD (w/Duet Accomp.)	Cahn	2
58-37	VIENNESE WALTZ	Gould	3